© 2002 by Barbour Publishing, Inc.

ISBN 1-58660-461-9

Cover image © Getty One

Published by Barbour Books, an imprint of Barbour Publishing, Inc., P.O. Box 719, Uhrichsville, Ohio 44683, www.barbourbooks.com

 Member of the
Evangelical Christian
Publishers Association

Printed in China.
5 4 3 2 1

CONGRATULATIONS!

LARISSA NYGREN

CONTENTS

YOU DID IT!

Congratulations on this day of celebration!

I have fought a good fight,
I have finished my course,
I have kept the faith.

2 TIMOTHY 4:7 KJV

Life affords no greater pleasure than overcoming obstacles.

AUTHOR UNKNOWN

Veni, Vidi, Vici. I came. I saw. I conquered.

JULIUS CAESAR

Nothing great was ever achieved without enthusiasm.

RALPH WALDO EMERSON

That man is a success who has lived well, laughed often, and loved much; who has gained the respect of intelligent men and the love of children; who has filled his niche and accomplished his task; who leaves the world better than he found it, whether by improved poppy, a perfect poem, or a rescued soul; who never lacked appreciation of earth's beauty or failed to express it; who looked for the best in others and gave the best he had.

ROBERT LOUIS STEVENSON

Four steps to achievement:
1. Plan purposefully.
2. Prepare prayerfully.
3. Proceed positively.
4. Pursue persistently.

WILLIAM A. WARD

*Thou shalt ever joy at eventide
if you spend the day fruitfully.*

THOMAS À KEMPIS

Just look what you've achieved!

People who soar are those who refuse to sit back, sigh, and wish things would change. They neither complain of their lot nor passively dream of some distant ship coming in. Rather, they visualize in their minds that they are not quitters; they will not allow life's circumstances to push them down and hold them under.

CHARLES R. SWINDOLL

*The world cares very little about
what a man or woman knows;
it is what the man or woman is able to do that counts.*

BOOKER T. WASHINGTON

Your work has paid off!

Every great achievement
was once considered impossible.

AUTHOR UNKNOWN

When love and skill work together expect a masterpiece.

JOHN RUSKIN

The only place where success comes before work
is in the dictionary.

VIDAL SASSOON

FATHER,

There were times when I thought this day would never arrive, times when the celebration seemed so far down the road. But You showed me the way and led me down the right path. I couldn't have done it without Your guidance and strength, Lord. You surrounded me with those You knew would help me turn my dreams into reality. You changed my heart, giving me determination and stability. Your will became mine, and Your power moved through me, ensuring my success. So my achievement is because of You, Father!

I look forward to the future with great anticipation because I know that You are in control, now and forever. Amen.

GOD IS GREAT!

You have not done this alone. . . .
God has done it for you!
Praise be to our wonderful Lord for His bountiful blessings!

We can do all things with the grace of God,
which He never refuses to them who ask it earnestly.
Knock, persevere in knocking,
and I answer for it that He will open it to you.

BROTHER LAWRENCE

When God calls a man, He does not repent of it. God does not, as many friends do, love one day, and hate another; or as princes, who make their subjects favorites, and afterwards throw them into prison. This is the blessedness of a saint; his condition admits of no alteration. God's call is founded on His decree, and His decree is immutable. Acts of grace cannot be reversed. God blots out His people's sins, but not their names.

THOMAS WATSON

Our motto must continue to be perseverance. And ultimately I trust the Almighty will crown our efforts with success.

WILLIAM WILBERFORCE

*Remember to thank Him for
the wonders He has worked in your life. . . .*

God gave you a gift of 86,400 seconds today.
Have you used one to say "thank you"?

WILLIAM ARTHUR WARD

*If the only prayer you said in your whole life was
"Thank You," that would suffice.*

MEISTER ECKHART

Count your blessings instead of your crosses,
Count your gains instead of your losses.
Count your joys instead of your woes,
Count your friends instead of your foes.
Count your health instead of your wealth.

IRISH BLESSING

Give thanks in all circumstances.

1 THESSALONIANS 5:18 NIV

Be on the lookout for mercies.
The more we look for them,
the more of them we will see. . . .
Better to lose count while naming your blessings
than to lose your blessings to counting your troubles.

AUTHOR UNKNOWN

Gratitude is the praise we offer God:
for teachers kind, benefactors never to be forgotten,
for all those who have advantaged me. . .
for all these and all others which I know, which I know not, open,
hidden, remembered, and forgotten.

LANCELOT ANDREWES

Where there is great love there are always miracles.

WILLA CATHER

*God loves us not because of who we are,
but because of who He is.*

AUTHOR UNKNOWN

Do you want to know what our Lord meant in all this?
Learn it well.
Love was what He meant.
Who showed it to you? Love.
Why did He show it? Out of Love.
So I was taught that love was what our Lord meant.

JULIAN OF NORWICH

Love Divine, all love excelling,
Joy of heaven to earth come down;
Fix in us thy humble dwelling;
All Thy faithful mercies crown.

CHARLES WESLEY

FATHER,

Thank You for this celebration, for the gathering of family and friends, for the love and support that is abounding around me. Sometimes, Lord, I forget the most important reason to be thankful—You. You are my reason to celebrate, my reason to love, my reason to share joy. And You are all the reason I need. Thank You, Lord, for being the reason. Amen.

THE SWEET SMELL OF SUCCESS!

The differences between a successful person
and others is not a lack of strength,
not a lack of knowledge,
but rather in a lack of will.

AUTHOR UNKNOWN

The secret of success is the constancy of purpose.

BENJAMIN DISRAELI

To persevere is to succeed.

THOMAS SUTCLIFFE MORT

Most men succeed because they are determined to.

GEORGE ALLEN

Don't aim for success if you want it;
just do what you love and believe in,
and it will come naturally.

DAVID FROST

The elevator to success is out of order.
You'll have to use the stairs. . .one step at a time.

JOE GIRARD

Character cannot be developed in ease and quiet.
Only through experience of trial and suffering
can the soul be strengthened, ambition inspired,
and success achieved.

HELEN KELLER

*I cannot give you the formula for success,
but I can give you the formula for failure,
which is:
Try to please everybody.*

HERBERT B. SWOPE

People become really quite remarkable when
they start thinking that they can do things.
When they believe in themselves
they have the first secret of success.

NORMAN VINCENT PEALE

*Success consists of getting up
just one more time than you fall.*

OLIVER GOLDSMITH

I owe my success to having listened respectfully
to the very best advice,
and then going away
and doing the exact opposite.

G. K. CHESTERTON

*God gave us two ends—
one to sit on and one to think with.
Success depends on which one you use;
heads, you win—tails, you lose.*

ANONYMOUS

THE LUSTER
OF LIFE

Thank you, Lord, for giving me life
and for helping me live it to the fullest!

I have come that they may have life,
and that they may have it more abundantly.

JOHN 10:10 NKJV

Today is a gift.
That's why it's called the present!

AUTHOR UNKNOWN

No man is a failure who is enjoying life.

WILLIAM FEATHER

CONGRATULATIONS!

*The tragedy of life is not that it ends so soon,
but that we wait so long to begin it.*

ANONYMOUS

Often people attempt to live their lives backwards—they try to have more things, or more money, in order to do more of what they want, so they will be happier. The way it actually works is the reverse. You must first be who you really are, then do what you need to do, in order to have what you want.

MARGARET YOUNG

*If you're climbing the ladder of life,
you go rung by rung, one step at a time. . . .
Sometimes you don't think you're progressing
until you step back
and see how high you've really gone.*

DONNY OSMOND

There are only two ways to live your life.
One is as though nothing is a miracle.
The other is as though everything is a miracle.

ALBERT EINSTEIN

*To be alive, to be able to see, to walk. . .
it's all a miracle.
I have adapted the technique of
living from miracle to miracle.*

ARTHUR RUBINSTEIN

Life is a great and wondrous mystery,
and the only thing we know that we have for sure is
what is right here right now. Don't miss it.

LEO BUSCAGLIA

*How we spend our days is, of course,
how we spend our lives.*

ANNIE DILLARD

If we are ever to enjoy life,
now is the time, not tomorrow or next year. . . .
Today should always be our most wonderful day.

THOMAS DREIER

*Life is all memory except for
the one present moment that goes by you
so quick you can hardly catch it going.*

TENNESSEE WILLIAMS

I learned that one can never go back,
that one should not ever go back—
that the essence of life is going forward.
Life is really a one-way street, isn't it?

AGATHA CHRISTIE

*Whatever you do,
do all to the glory of God.*

1 CORINTHIANS 10:31 NKJV

The value of life lies not in the length of days,
but in the use we make of them.

MICHEL DE MONTAIGNE

Take the life that you have and give it your best,
Think positive, be happy, let God do the rest,
Take the challenges that life has laid at your feet,
Take pride and be thankful for each one you meet,
To yourself give forgiveness if you stumble and fall,
Take each day that is dealt you and give it your all,
Take the love that you're given and return it with care,
Have faith that when needed it will always be there,
Take time to find the beauty in the things that you see,
Take life's simple pleasures, let them set your heart free.

AUTHOR UNKNOWN

Life is a journey, not a destination.

AUTHOR UNKNOWN

GOD,

I can only pray that I'm living a life that is pleasing to You. You have given me everything and continue to be with me each step of the way, through my every journey. May I give You my all and never forget that You have placed me where I am for a reason, and that reason is to show Your love. May my life be in some way a reflection of You, Lord, that others may see in me Your light and heart. Amen.

YOU BELIEVED IN YOUR DREAMS!

It is a daring thing to follow your dreams. . . .
This in itself is reason to celebrate!

"There's no use trying," [Alice] said.
"One can't believe impossible things."
"I daresay you haven't had much practice," said the Queen.
"When I was your age, I always did it for half an hour a day.
Why, sometimes I've believed as many as
six impossible things before breakfast."

LEWIS CARROLL, *Alice in Wonderland*

*It is difficult to say what is impossible,
for the dream of yesterday is the hope of today
and the reality of tomorrow.*

ROBERT H. GODDARD

A dream is in the mind of the believer,
and in the hands of the doer.
You are not given a dream,
without being given the power to make it come true.

ANONYMOUS

*If you have built castles in the air,
your work need not be lost; that is where they should be.
Now put the foundations under them.*

HENRY DAVID THOREAU

Consider it pure joy, my brothers, whenever you face trials of many kinds, because you know that the testing of your faith develops perseverance. Perseverance must finish its work so that you may be mature and complete, not lacking anything.

JAMES 1:2–4 NIV

A champion is someone who gets up even when he can't.

AUTHOR UNKNOWN

Most of the important things in the world have been accomplished by people who have kept on trying when there seemed to be no hope at all.

DALE CARNEGIE

Dreams do come true, if we only wish hard enough.
You can have anything in life if
you will sacrifice everything else for it.
"What will you have?" says God.
"Pray for it and take it."

JAMES M. BARRIE

When your heart is in your dreams,
no request is too extreme.

JIMINY CRICKET

The future belongs to those who believe in
the beauty of their dreams.

ELEANOR ROOSEVELT

31

The Best is Yet to Come...

I love the theater. One of the things I find most thrilling in life is taking small pieces. . .actors, written words, an empty stage, the love of entertaining. . .and putting them together to form something great, watching something so raw become so polished, so full of heart. Especially moving is seeing the delight in the eyes of those in the audience who have in some way been touched by the big picture. Yet as quickly as a show opens, so it closes. The goal you've been working toward so hard in this part of your life is suddenly over, and it's easy to feel let down, unfulfilled, that your moment in the sun has passed. That feeling may come to each of us after any great accomplishment.

But what we must remember is that there will be more moments in the sun, thanks to the plan that God has for each of us. When one dream fades away, another will appear. The small miracles and blessings that God surrounds us with every day of our lives will come to light. And as He reminds us, the best is yet to come. Each of us is a part of something great because we are a part of Him. Each of us can feel His love and know that we are a part of the "big picture" that is touching the lives of everyone around us. And when this play is done, we will join Him for all eternity.

So rejoice in this time of celebration!
Rejoice in the fact that
this is just the beginning,
and the best is yet to come!

FOLLOW
YOUR DREAMS!

Let God lead the way. . . .

The future is
as bright as the promises of God.

ADONIRAM JUDSON

Do not follow where the path may lead.
Go instead where there is no path and leave a trail.

RALPH WALDO EMERSON

In the confrontation between the stream and the rock,
the stream always wins—
not through strength but through perseverance.

AUTHOR UNKNOWN

Trying times are no times to quit trying.

AUTHOR UNKNOWN

Be of good cheer. Do not think of today's failure, but of the success that may come tomorrow. You have set yourselves a difficult task, but you will succeed if you persevere; and you will find joy in overcoming obstacles. Remember, no effort that we make to attain something beautiful is ever lost.

HELEN KELLER

Never give in, never give in, never, never, never, never—
in nothing, great or small, large or petty—
never give in except to convictions of honor and good sense.

WINSTON CHURCHILL

It does not matter how slowly you go,
so long as you do not stop.

CONFUCIUS

Don't wait for your ship to come;
swim out to it.

ANONYMOUS

Hitch your wagon to a star.

RALPH WALDO EMERSON

36

Reach high, for stars lie hidden in your soul.
Dream deep, for every dream precedes the goal.

PAMELA VAULL STARR

You see things; and you say "Why?"
But I dream things that never were; and I say "Why not?"

GEORGE BERNARD SHAW

All dreams can come true—
if we have the courage to pursue them.

WALT DISNEY

Always listen to experts.
They tell you what can't be done and why. Then do it.

ROBERT HEINLEIN

37

Most people never run far enough on their first wind,
to find out if they've got a second.
Give your dreams all you've got
and you'll be amazed at the energy that comes out of you.

WILLIAM JAMES

*Why not go out on a limb?
Isn't that where the fruit is?*

FRANK SCULLY

A piece of the miracle process
has been reserved for each of us.

JIM ROHN

To accomplish great things,
we must not only act,
but also dream;
not only plan, but also believe.

ANATOLE FRANCE

*If you can't excel with talent,
triumph with effort.*

DAVE WEINBAUM

Never part with your illusions.
Without dreams you may continue to exist,
but you have ceased to live.

MARK TWAIN

CONGRATULATIONS!

I have learned at least this by my experiments:
that if one advances confidently
in the direction of his dreams and endeavors,
to live the life which he has imagined,
he will meet with a success unexpected in common hours.

HENRY DAVID THOREAU

FATHER,

Thank You for all the blessings You've bestowed upon me, for giving me dreams to follow, and for leading the way. I know that this is only the beginning, Lord, that there is much more of this journey to go. And I know that every moment won't be as grand as this one, but I will learn from each lesson You teach me. I will take every success and failure alike and apply the principles I've learned from Your Word. Then each new day will be a celebration because I will spend them growing closer to You!

Thank you, God, for this blessed occasion.

In Your Name, I pray and rejoice! Amen.